The Christmas Story
ACCORDING TO LUKE

For unto us a child is born, unto us a son is given:
and the government shall be upon His shoulder:
and His name shall be called Wonderful, Counselor,
The mighty God, The everlasting Father, The Prince of Peace.

Of the increase of His government and peace there shall
be no end, upon the throne of David, and upon His kingdom,
to order it, and to establish it with judgment and with justice
from henceforth even for ever. The zeal of the LORD of hosts
will perform this.

Isaiah 9:6–7

The story of the birth

of Jesus the Savior

is presented to

_____

_____

by

_____

_____

_____

The Christmas Story

According to LUKE

Illustrated by DONALD KUEKER
for Concordia Publishing House
with text from the King James Version of the Bible

The LORD Himself shall give you a sign; Behold, a virgin shall
conceive, and bear a son, and shall call His name Immanuel.

Isaiah 7:14

CONCORDIA PUBLISHING HOUSE • SAINT LOUIS

In the days of Herod, the king of Judea …

the angel Gabriel was sent from God unto a city of Galilee,
named Nazareth, to a virgin espoused to a man whose name
was Joseph, of the house of David; and the virgin's name was Mary.

And the angel came in unto her, and said,
Hail, thou that art highly favored, the Lord is with thee:
blessed are thou among women.

And when she saw him, she was troubled at his saying,
and cast in her mind what manner of salutation this should be.

And the angel said unto her, Fear not, Mary: for thou hast
found favor with God.

And, behold, thou shalt conceive in thy womb, and bring
forth a son, and shalt call His name JESUS.

He shall be great, and shall be called the Son of the Highest:
and the Lord God shall give unto Him the throne of His father
David: And He shall reign over the house of Jacob for ever;
and of His kingdom there shall be no end.

Then said Mary unto the angel, How shall this be, seeing I know not a man?

And the angel answered and said unto her, The Holy Ghost shall come upon thee, and the power of the Highest shall overshadow thee: therefore also that holy thing which shall be born of thee shall be called the Son of God.

And, behold, thy cousin Elisabeth, she hath also conceived a son in her old age; and this is the sixth month with her, who was called barren.

For with God nothing shall be impossible.

And Mary said, Behold the handmaid of the Lord; be it unto me according to thy word. And the angel departed from her.

And it came to pass in those days,

that there went out a decree from Caesar Augustus, that all the world should be taxed.

(And this taxing was first made when Cyrenius was governor of Syria.)

And all went to be taxed, every one into his own city.

And Joseph also went up from Galilee, out of the city of Nazareth, into Judea,

unto the city of David, which is called Bethlehem,
(because he was of the house and lineage of David,)
  To be taxed with Mary his espoused wife, being great with child.

And so it was, that, while they were there, the days were accomplished that she should be delivered.

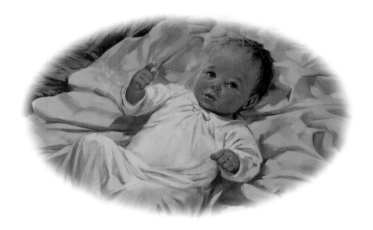

And she brought forth her firstborn son,

and wrapped Him in swaddling clothes, and laid Him in a manger; because there was no room for them in the inn.

And there were in the same country shepherds
abiding in the field, keeping watch over their flock by night.

And, lo, the angel of the Lord came upon them,
and the glory of the Lord shone round about them;
and they were sore afraid.

And the angel said unto them, Fear not: for, behold, I bring you good tidings of great joy, which shall be to all people.

For unto you is born this day in the city of David a Saviour, which is Christ the Lord.

And this shall be a sign unto you; Ye shall find the babe wrapped in swaddling clothes, lying in a manger.

And suddenly there was with the angel a multitude of the heavenly host praising God, and saying,

Glory to God in the highest, and on earth peace, good will toward men.

And it came to pass, as the angels were gone away
from them into heaven, the shepherds said one to another,
Let us now go even unto Bethlehem, and see this thing which
is come to pass, which the Lord hath made known unto us.

And they came with haste, and found Mary
and Joseph, and the babe lying in a manger.

And when they had seen it, they made known abroad
the saying which was told them concerning this child.

And all they that heard it wondered at those things which
were told them by the shepherds.

But Mary kept all these things, and pondered them in her heart.

And the shepherds returned, glorifying and praising God for all the things that they had heard and seen, as it was told unto them.

Luke 2:1–20

Concordia
Publishing House

Published 2004 by Concordia Publishing House
Copyright © 1993 Concordia Publishing House
3558 S. Jefferson Avenue
St. Louis, MO 63118-3968

Illustrations by Donald Kueker © Concordia Publishing House

Scripture quotations are taken from the King James or Authorized Version of the Bible.

Manufactured in the United States of America

1   2   3   4   5   6   7   8   9   10   13 12 11 10 09 08 07 06 05 04